1

Concepts in SCIENCE

Concepts in SCIENCE

1

PAUL F. BRANDWEIN

ELIZABETH K. COOPER

PAUL E. BLACKWOOD

ELIZABETH B. HONE

HARCOURT, BRACE & WORLD, INC.

New York   Chicago   Atlanta   Dallas   Burlingame

Picture Credits

Cover: Harbrace Photo. *Text:* p. vi and 1, David W. Nilsson, Shostal; p. 9, Pastner, F.P.G.; p. 19, L. Willinger, F.P.G.; p. 29, 39, Harbrace Photo; p. 49, Rapho Guillumette; p. 61, Harbrace Photo; p. 75, Ylla, Rapho Guillumette; p. 95, D. W. Thornton, National Audubon Society; p. 117, Dennis Halliman, Alpha; p. 127, American Museum of Natural History; p. 143, Hollyman, Photo Researchers.

Illustrators

Wayne Blickenstaff, Charles Liese, John Ballantine, Darrell Sweet,
Paul Granger, Gabe Keith, Ann Brewster, Robert Jones

CONTENTS

MAKING THINGS MOVE   1

MOVING FASTER   9

UP AND DOWN   19

HOT AND COLD   29

CLOUDY OR SUNNY   39

LIGHT AND DARK   49

PLANTS AND MORE PLANTS   61

ANIMALS AND MORE ANIMALS   75

LIVING THINGS GROW   95

WE GROW   117

LONG, LONG AGO   127

CHANGES WE SEE   143

MAKING THINGS MOVE

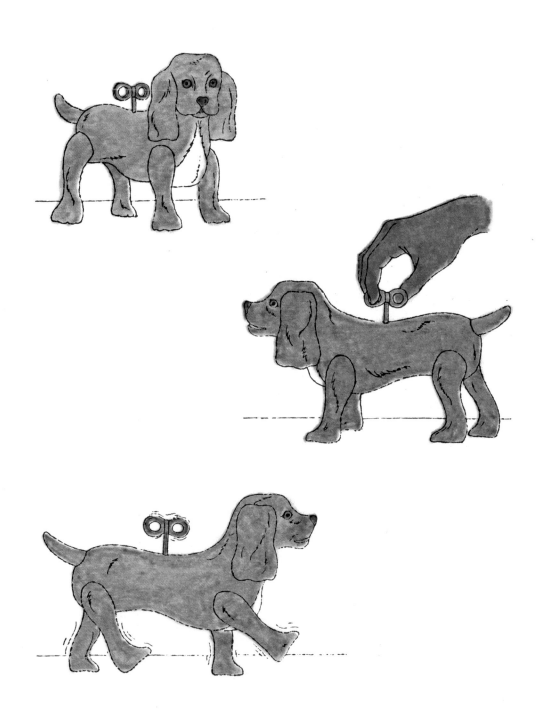

What makes the toy dog move?

What makes the real dog move?

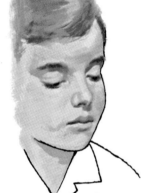

What makes it move?

4

What makes it move?

What makes it move?

What makes it move?

THE BIG IDEA

MOVING FASTER

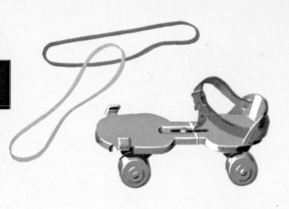

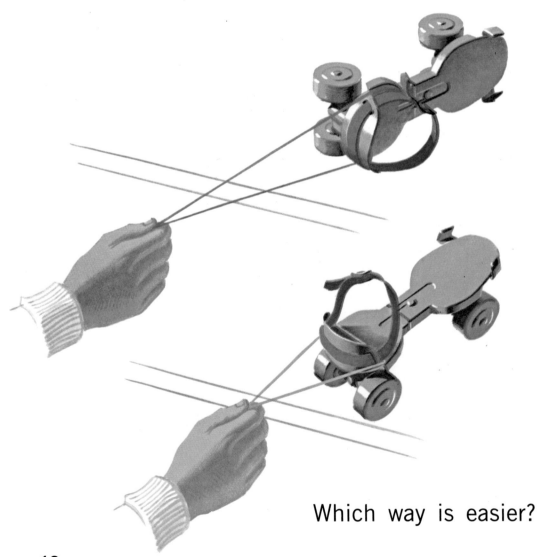

Which way is easier?

Which way is easier?

Which way is easier?

Which way is faster?

Which way is faster?

Which does more work?

Which does more work?

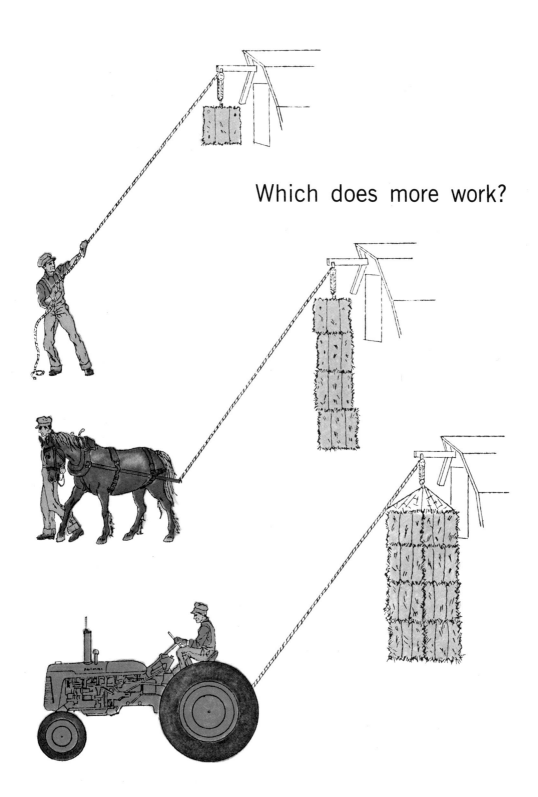

Which does more work?

17

THE BIG IDEA

UP AND DOWN

Why does the apple fall?

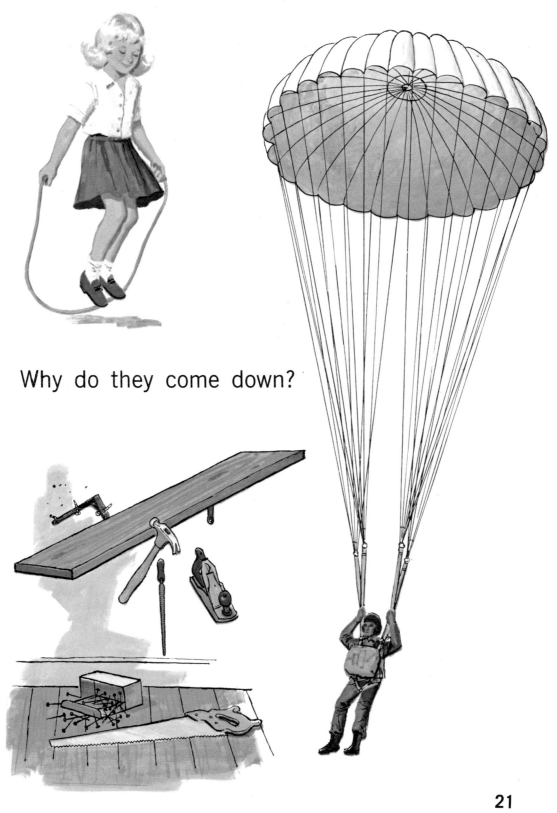

Why do they come down?

Why does the cat fall?
How does the cat get up?

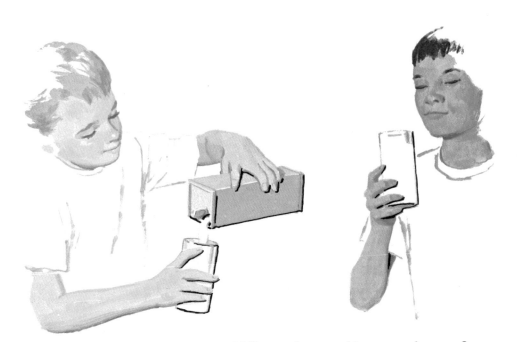

Why does it go down?

What makes them go up?

What lifts it up?

What makes it go up?

What can a magnet lift?

A magnet can do work.

THE BIG IDEA

HOT AND COLD

What is in the bag?

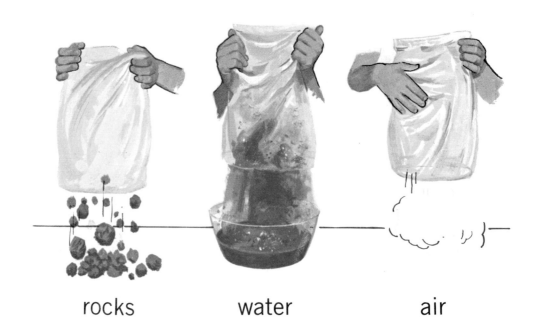

rocks   water   air

What is in the bag?

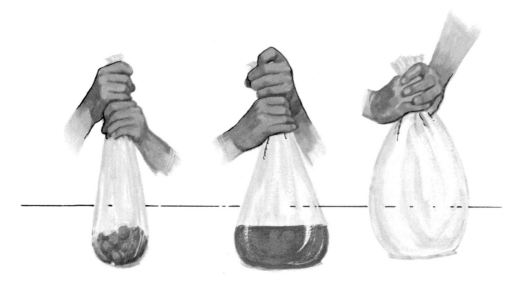

solid   liquid   gas

How does ice change?

What makes ice change?

What makes it change?

MILDRED E. LEARY
ELEMENTARY SUPERVISOR
NORTH ATTLEBOROUGH, MASS.

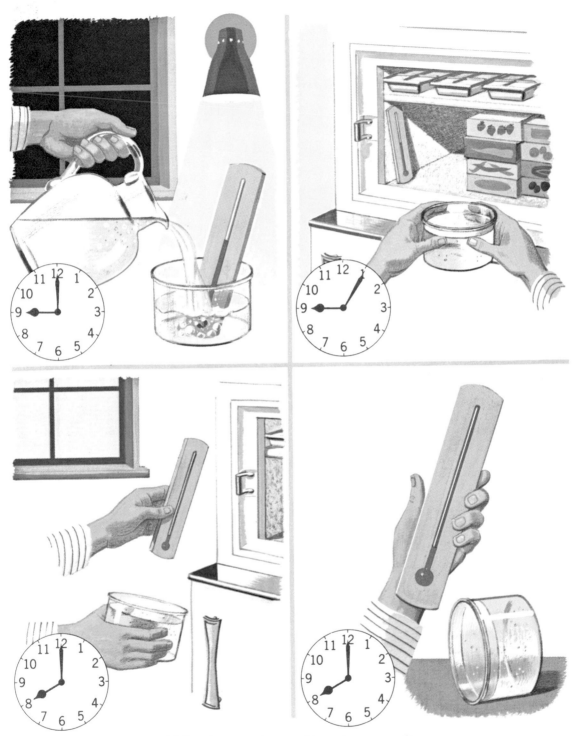

What makes it change?

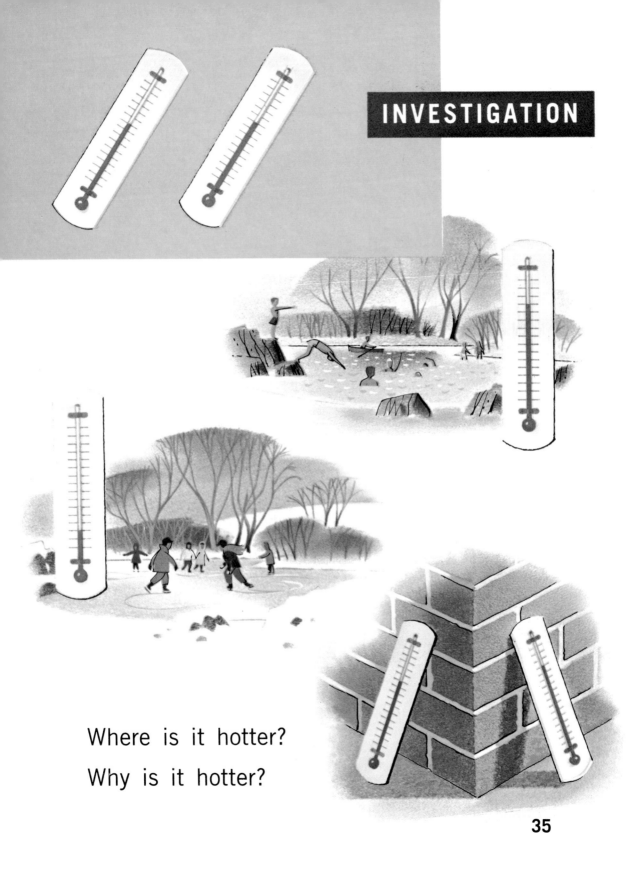

Where is it hotter?

Why is it hotter?

35

INVESTIGATION

Monday

Tuesday

10 drops of water

How many drops?

Which will dry faster?

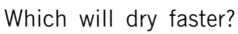

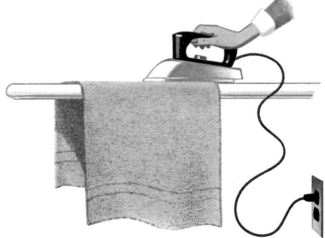

THE BIG IDEA

CLOUDY OR SUNNY

What makes the little cloud?

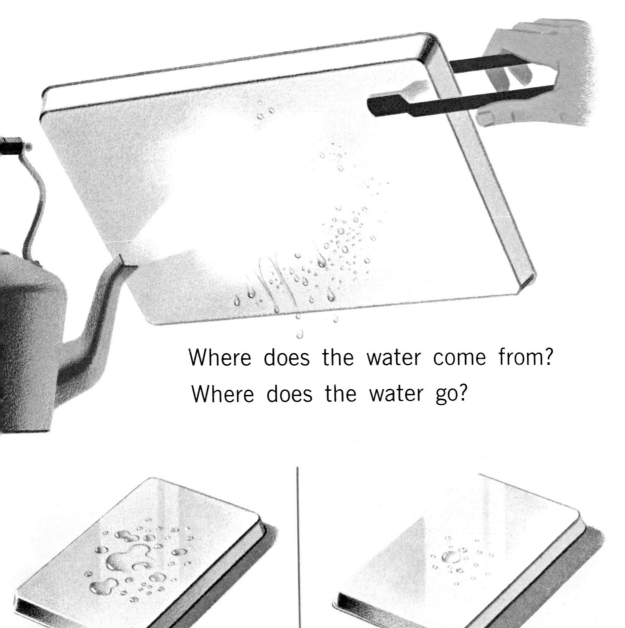

Where does the water come from?

Where does the water go?

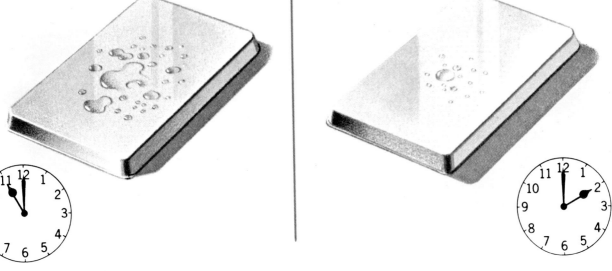

Where do the drops of water come from?

Where did the rain come from?

Will it rain?

Monday

Wednesday

Friday

What makes the difference?

44

What will happen to the water?

Why will it happen?

45

Where do clouds get water?

Where is it raining?

Which side of the mountain gets more rain?

THE BIG IDEA

water

cloud

fog

LIGHT AND DARK

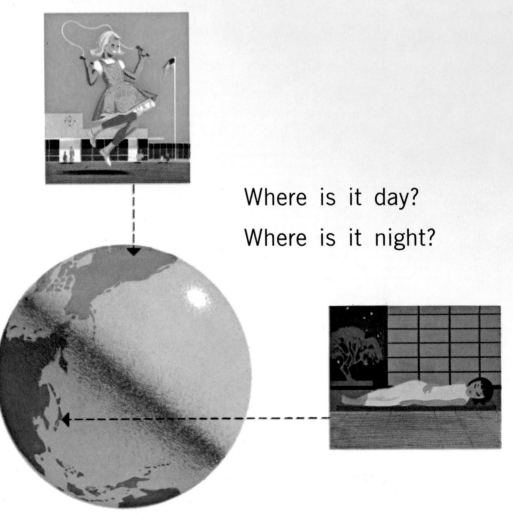

Where is it day?

Where is it night?

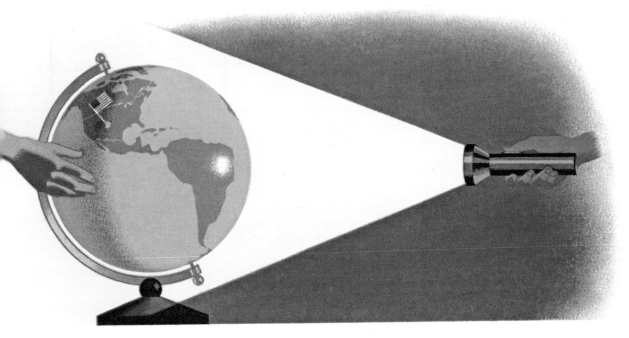

Night comes after day.

Day comes after night.

What does the Earth do?

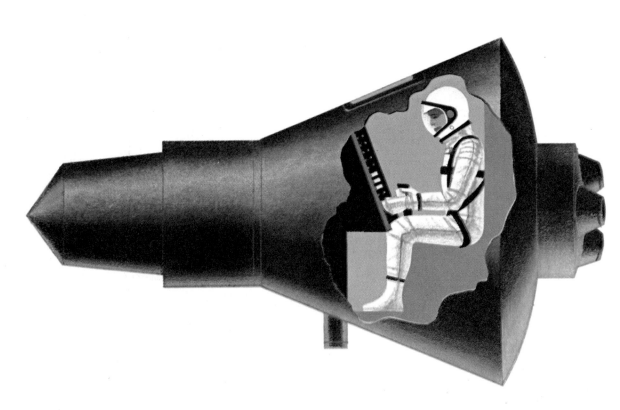

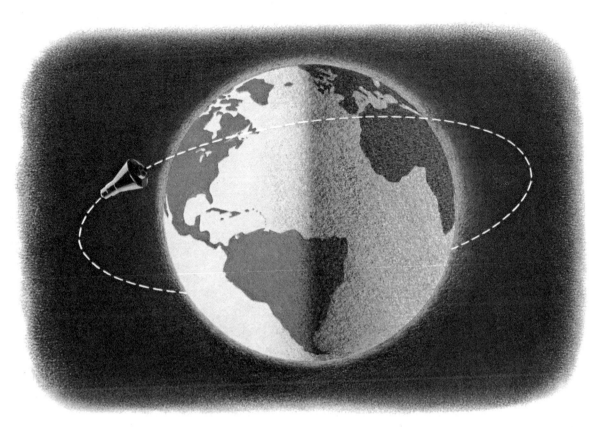

Where is it light?   Why?

Where is it dark?   Why?

Where does our light come from?

Why do we have shadows?

54

Where is the Sun?

Early morning

Noon

Early evening

Where does the Moon get its light?

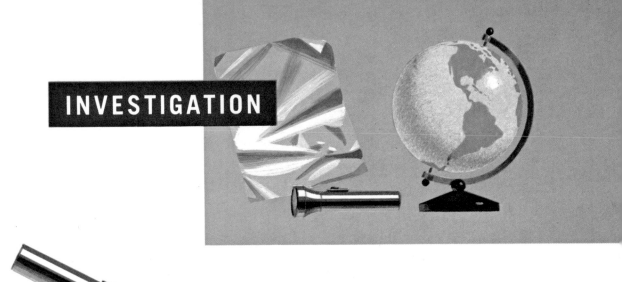

Why does the Moon shine?

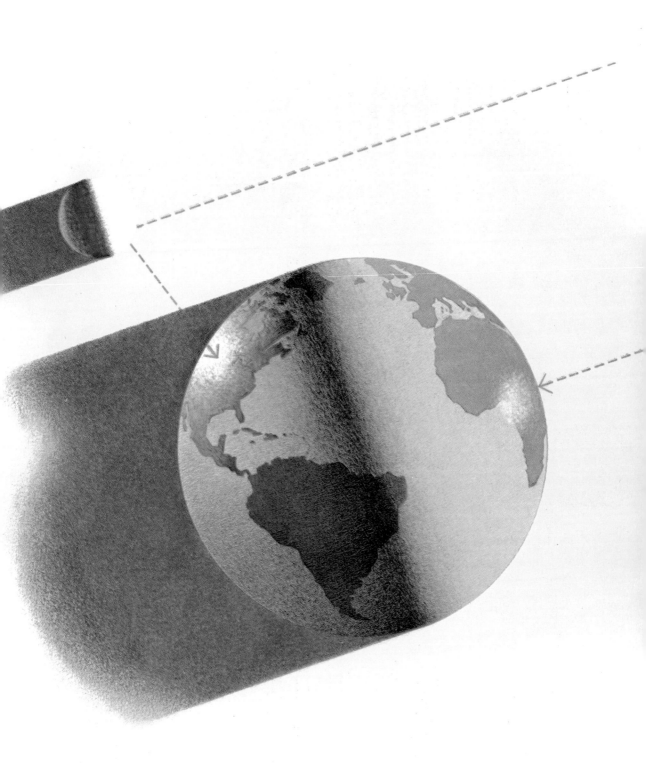

The Sun lights the Earth and the Moon.

THE BIG IDEA

PLANTS AND MORE PLANTS

Seeds come from a plant.

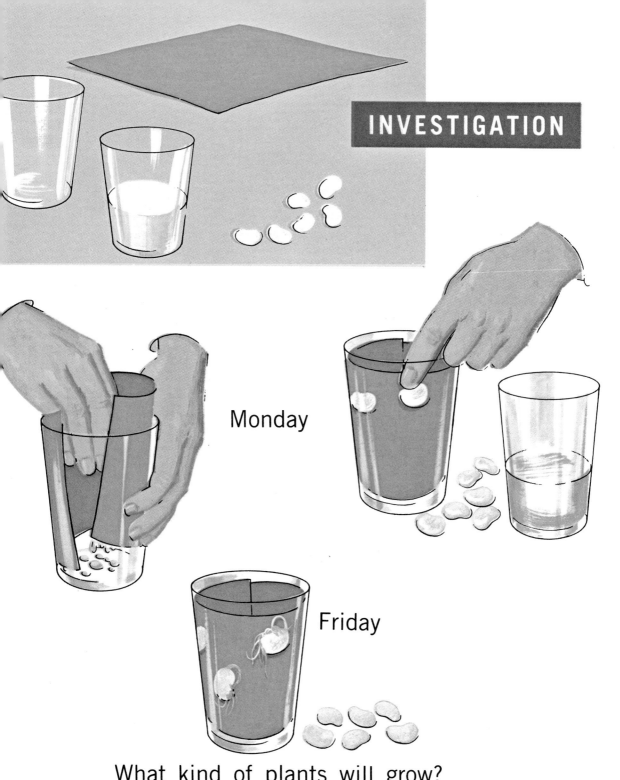

Monday

Friday

What kind of plants will grow?

What kinds of plants will grow?

What kinds of plants grew?

From what do they grow?

From what do they grow?

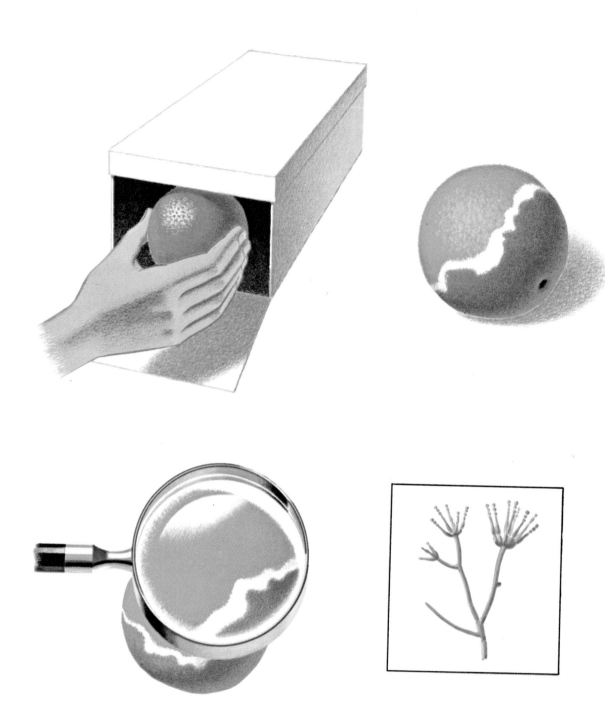

What grows on the orange?

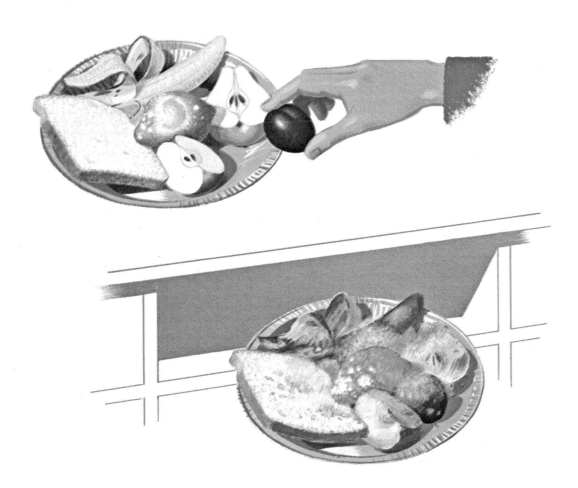

What kind of plants are growing?

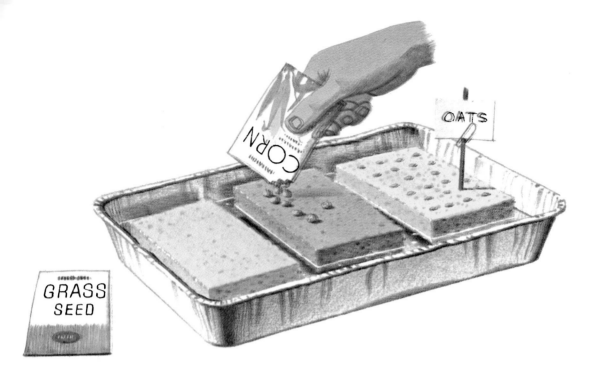

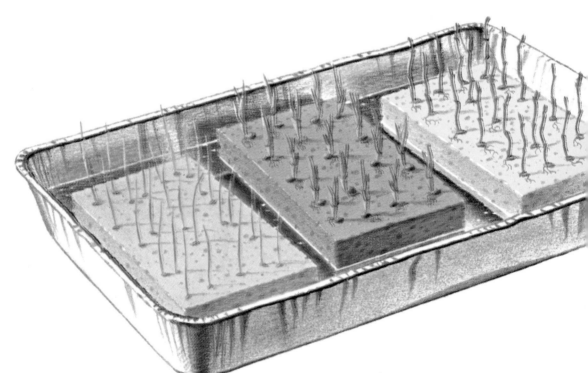

What kinds of plants are growing?

What kinds of plants will grow?

What is happening?

Why are they different?

THE BIG IDEA

peach

orange

cherry

pear

apple

ANIMALS AND MORE ANIMALS

Find the parent.

Find the parent.

Find the parent.

Find the parent.

Find the parent.

Find the parent.

Animals on the farm

Animals on the farm

Animals at the zoo

Animals at the zoo

Dog with puppies

Cat with kittens

blue jay

oriole

sparrow

robin

mockingbird

gold finch

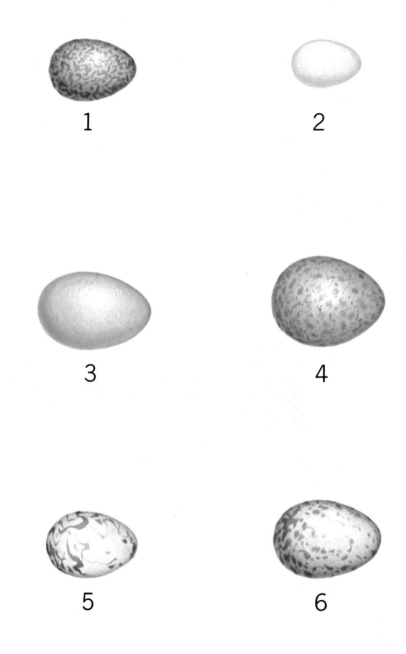

1

2

3

4

5

6

What kinds of birds will hatch?

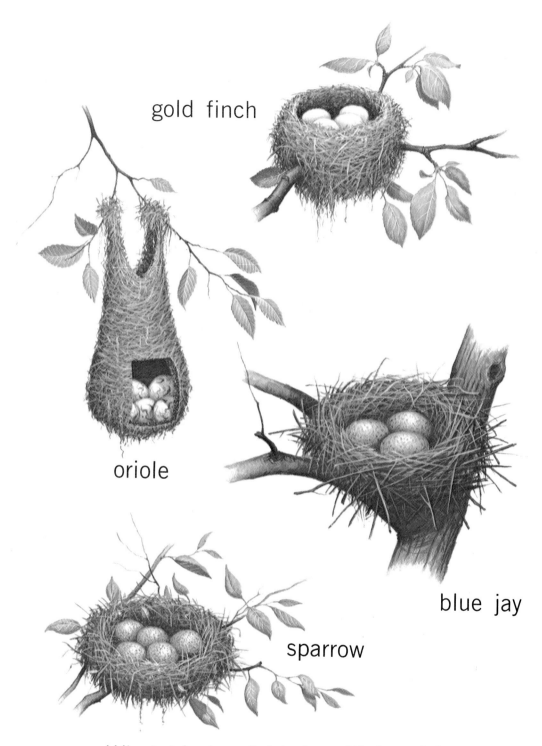

gold finch

oriole

blue jay

sparrow

What kinds of birds will hatch?

Robins

Four young robins are in the nest.

They are very hungry.

The mother robin feeds them.

The father feeds them, too.

The young robins eat and grow.

Soon they will fly.

Cowbirds

A cowbird does not make a nest.

It lays eggs in other birds' nests.

A cowbird laid eggs in a warbler's nest.

A warbler also laid eggs in the nest.

The warbler sat on all the eggs.

The warbler feeds all the young birds.

The young cowbirds grab most of the food.

They may push the warblers out of the nest.

THE BIG IDEA

LIVING THINGS GROW

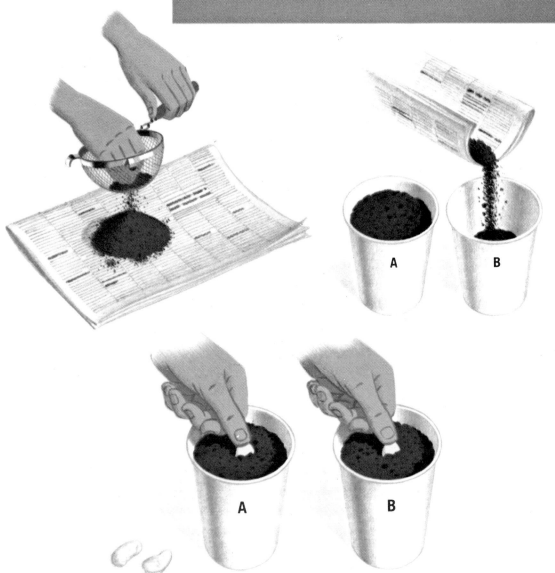

INVESTIGATION

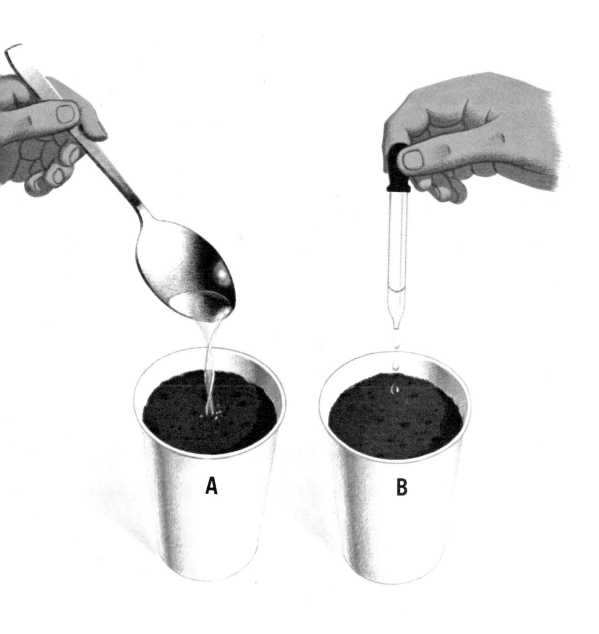

Give cup **A** 1 spoonful of water.

Give cup **B** 3 drops of water.

Do this every day.

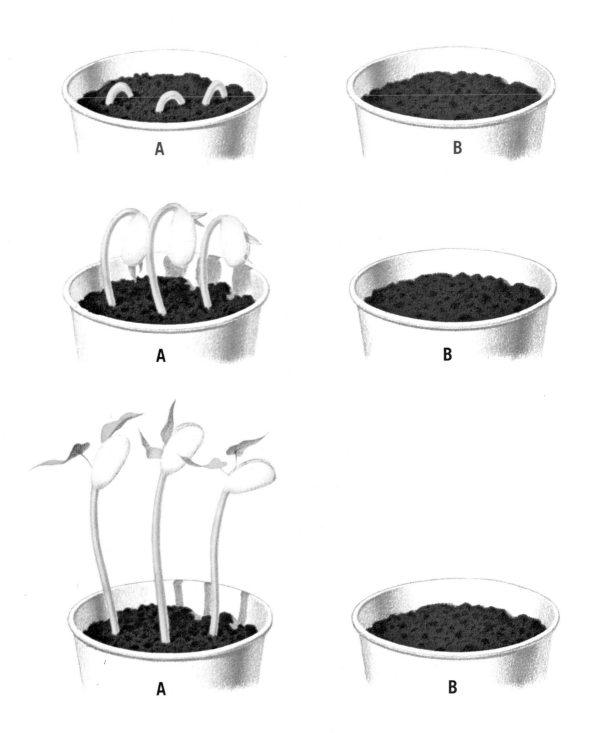

What makes the difference?

The plant has green leaves.

It has pink flowers.

It grows in the sunlight.

It gets water every day.

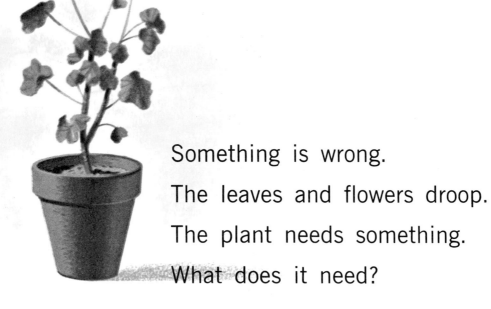

Something is wrong.

The leaves and flowers droop.

The plant needs something.

What does it need?

What makes the difference?

What makes the difference?

What makes the difference?

Mary had a little calf.
She led it to the pasture.
The calf fed on green grass.
He drank water from a stream.

At night the calf
came to the barn.
Mary brushed his coat
and fed him oats and hay.

Mary took her calf to the Fair.
The calf won a big blue ribbon.
It was the best calf in the Fair.

Put in the sand.

Put in the water.

In a few days
put in the plants.

In a few more days put in the fish and snails.

Taking Care of Your Aquarium

Keep the aquarium in the light.

Keep it away from the heat.

Feed the fish a little food each day.

Plants make their own food.

Do not feed the snails.

Snails find their own foods.

Snails help keep the aquarium clean.

You can help keep it clean, too.

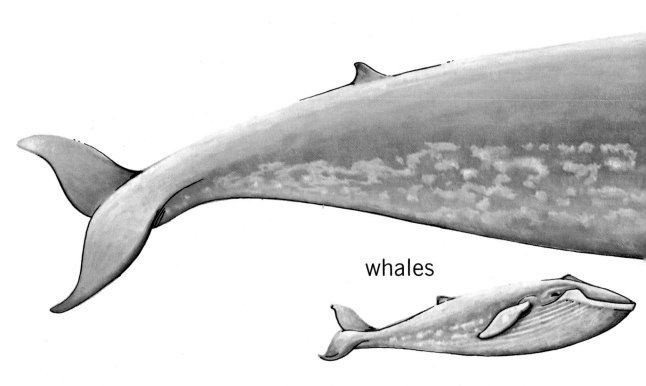

whales

Which young animal will grow biggest?

seals

penguins

horses

elephants

pigs

Large and small

Large and small puppies

Two Little Seeds

One seed came from an apple.

One seed came from a tomato.

The seeds were planted in the soil.

They sprouted and grew into plants.

Why did the plants grow?

Which one became a tree?

Why does one plant grow better?

Is something missing?

Is something wrong?

THE BIG IDEA

What do the robins need?

Is something wrong?

Greg and His Brother

Greg is six years old.

His brother is big and strong.

Greg watches his brother play baseball.

Greg wants to be big and strong.

He wants to be like his brother.

119

A good breakfast

A good lunch

A good dinner

Extra treats

Food gives you energy.

Food helps you grow.

How much do you weigh now?

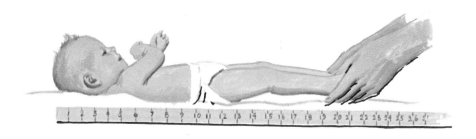

How tall are you now?

We are all in the same grade.

We are the same in some ways.

We are different in some ways.

We do not look alike.

We are not all the same size.

Some of us grow fast.

Some of us grow more slowly.

We all grow differently.

Which is more healthful?

LONG, LONG AGO

Something Like a Lizard

Long, long ago, the Earth was different.

It was very warm.

There were big swamps.

There were big forests of strange trees.

Strange animals lived on the land.

Some lived in the swamps.

Some of the animals looked like
giant lizards.

They were dinosaurs.

A dinosaur was a kind of reptile.

There are no dinosaurs alive today.

They died out long, long ago.

Some dinosaurs were nearly as big
as whales.

Others were as small as chickens.

Some could swim.

Some had mouths like ducks' bills.

Some had big horns on their heads.

Some had hard plates on their backs.

Some dinosaurs fed on plants that grew
in the forests and swamps.
Some dinosaurs fed on meat.
The meat-eaters killed other dinosaurs
to use for food.
Dinosaurs laid eggs.

The men dig for bones of a dinosaur.

How do we know about dinosaurs?

Something Like an Elephant

Long, long ago, a big animal lived.

It lived where some of us live today.

Its body was covered with hair.

It had a trunk like an elephant's.

Its two front teeth grew into long tusks.

It fed on trees and other plants.

It was a hairy mammoth.

Long, long ago men hunted mammoths.

They used mammoths for food.

They drew pictures of mammoths
on the walls of their caves.

There are no mammoths today.

They died out many, many years ago.

Mammoth in a Deep Freeze

One day a dog found a strange animal.

It was frozen in the earth.

Men dug away the ice and frozen earth.

They found part of a mammoth.

It had been frozen for many, many years.

How long will the insect stay the same?

Something Like a Cat

The sabertooth lived long, long ago.

It looked something like a cat.

It had two long, sharp teeth.

It used its teeth to kill other animals.

It used other animals for food.

A big animal came to drink.

Its feet stuck in the tar.

A hungry sabertooth jumped on the animal.

It fell off the animal and into the tar.

Both animals were caught.

They were caught for thousands of years.

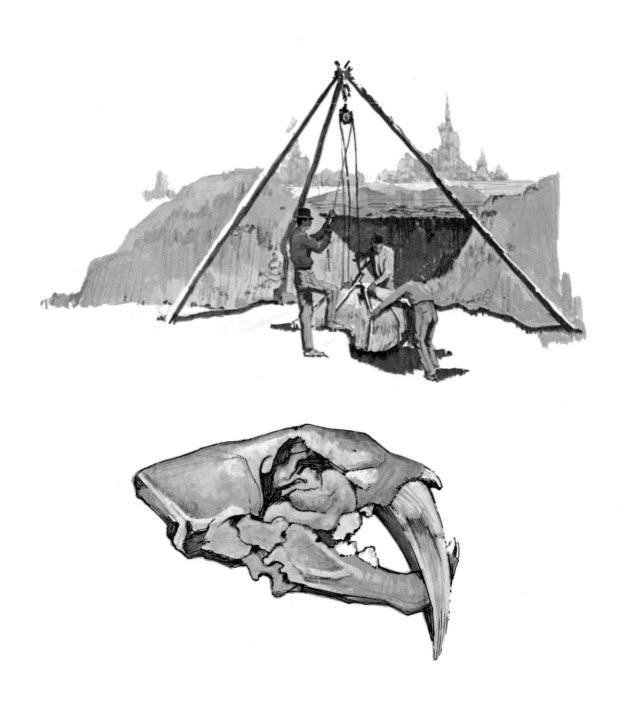

What do they find in the tar?

How do we know about the sabertooth?

THE BIG IDEA

Which animal was something like a lizard?

Which one was something like a cat?

Which one was something like an elephant?

Which one was a reptile?

Which one laid eggs?

Which two were mammals?

CHANGES WE SEE

Up and Down

I will throw my ball high.

I will make it touch a cloud.

I will throw it so high

it will never come down.

My ball goes up,

but it always comes down.

Many things come down.

Sand falls through my fingers.

Leaves fall from the trees.

Rocks roll down the hill.

Water runs down the hill.

Raindrops fall to the Earth.

Gravity pulls things to the Earth.

My energy sends the ball up,

and gravity pulls it down.

A Riddle

Hens lay eggs.

Chicks hatch out.

It takes twenty-one days for chicks
to hatch from eggs.

The chicks grow up.

Some grow up to become hens.

Some grow up to become roosters.

The hens lay more eggs.

More chicks hatch out.

They grow into hens and roosters.

Which came first,

the chicken or the egg?

Would you say the chicken came first?

Would you say the egg came first?

Would you say there is no first?

It just goes on and on and on and on.

Drops of water shine in the sunlight.

The water changes to water vapor.

The water vapor goes into the air.

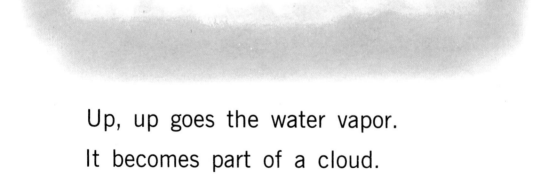

Up, up goes the water vapor.

It becomes part of a cloud.

Wind pushes the cloud across the sky.

The cloud gets cold. It rains.

The rain falls to the Earth.

The Sun comes out.

The Sun shines on the water.

New clouds form. It rains again.

It just goes on and on and on and on.

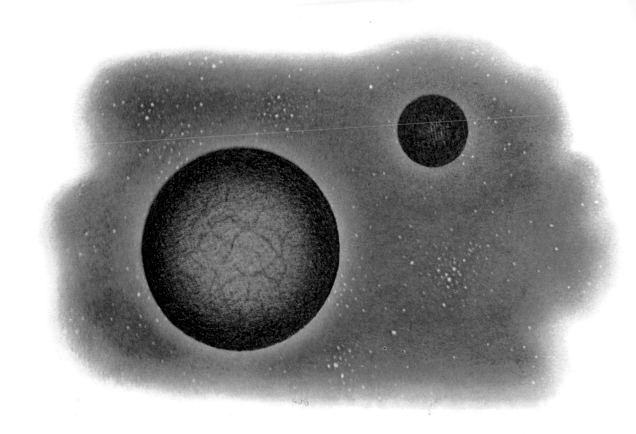

What If?

What if the Sun stopped shining?

The Earth would have no sunlight.
We would have no moonlight.

Everything would be dark and cold.

All the water would change to ice.

Green plants would die.

Animals would have no food

if the Sun stopped shining.

But the Sun does shine!
Because it does,
we have warm, sunny days.
We have moonlight at night.
We have clouds and rain.
We have grass and trees.
We have food from green plants.
We have many kinds of animals.
There is life on the Earth
because the Sun shines.

Just Imagine

Just imagine that you take a trip.

You take a trip to the Moon.

When you get near the Moon,

gravity pulls you down.

Does the Sun shine on the Moon?

Is there any water or air?

Are there any plants or animals?

Soon men may land on the Moon.

Watch for it.

WORDS USED IN CHILD'S TEXT

work, 15	Earth, 51	gold finch, 89
investigation, 25	light, 53	hatch, 90
magnet, 26	dark, 53	nest, 92
water, 30	shadow, 54	egg, 93
air, 30	Moon, 57	warbler, 93
rock, 30	plant, 62	cowbird, 93
solid, 31	seed, 62	leaves, 99
liquid, 31	grass, 70	*calf, 105
gas, 31	parent, 76	aquarium, 108
drop, 36	puppy, 86	whales, 110
cloud, 40	blue jay, 88	seals, 110
fog, 48	oriole, 88	penguins, 110
Sun, 50	sparrow, 88	elephant, 110
day, 50	robin, 89	tomato, 114
night, 50	mockingbird, 89	sprouted, 114

*optional

WORDS INTRODUCED IN TEACHER'S EDITION

food, 2	melt, 32	grass, 70	cow, 83
energy, 2	heat, 33	fruit, 71	rabbit, 83
science, 3	thermometer, 33	tree, 72	pig, 83
electricity, 4	degree, 34	potato eye, 73	horse, 83
fuel, 5	temperature, 35	chicken, 76	sheep, 83
gasoline, 5	water vapor, 36	bird, 76	goat, 83
wind, 6	evaporate, 36	turtle, 77	mammal, 83
wheels, 11	droplet, 41	snake, 77	*colt, 83
friction, 12	fog, 42	lizard, 77	*lamb, 83
gears, 16	rain, 43	reptile, 77	*kid, 83
pulling, 17	Sun, 44	scales, 77	*sow, 83
pulley, 17	desert, 47	insect, 78	fur, 84-85
gravity, 21	rotates, 51	grasshopper, 78	zoo, 84-85
Earth, 21	space, 52	caterpillar, 79	gazelle, 84-85
force, 23	astronaut, 52	cocoon, 79	lion, 84-85
*weight, 23	*capsule, 52	moth, 79	bear, 84-85
*weigh, 23	reflect, 56	fish, 80	kangaroo, 84-85
lift, 24	flower, 62	salmon, 80	giraffe, 84-85
push, 25	seed pod, 62	gills, 80	zebra, 84-85
rocket, 25	sprout, 63	tadpole, 81	dog, 86-87
opposite, 25	soil, 64	frog, 81	cat, 86-87
metal, 26	roots, 66	lungs, 81	kitten, 86-87
iron, 26	stem, 66	*toads, 81	dachshund, 113
steel, 26	leaves, 66	*salamanders, 81	great Dane, 113
ice, 32	mold, 68	*amphibians, 81	weeds, 115

*optional

154